A Note c

RUDOLF STEINER (1861–1925) called his spiritual philosophy 'anthroposophy', which can be understood as 'wisdom of the human being'. A highly developed seer, Steiner based his work on direct knowledge and perception of spiritual dimensions. He initiated a modern and universal 'science of spirit', accessible to anybody willing to exercise clear and unprejudiced thinking.

From his spiritual investigations, Steiner provided suggestions for the renewal of many activities, including education—both general and special—agriculture, medicine, economics, architecture, science, philosophy, religion and the arts. Today there are literally thousands of schools, clinics, farms and other organizations doing practical work based on his principles. His many published works (writings and lectures) also feature his research into the spiritual nature of the human being, the evolution of the world and humanity, and methods of personal development. Steiner wrote some 30 books and delivered over 6,000 lectures across Europe. In 1924 he founded the General Anthroposophical Society, which today has branches throughout the world.

Also in the *Meditations* series:

MEDITATIONS
for the Dead

Connecting to those who have Died

Rudolf Steiner

Edited and translated
by Matthew Barton

Sophia Books

An imprint of Rudolf Steiner Press

Sophia Books
An imprint of Rudolf Steiner Press
Hillside House, The Square
Forest Row, East Sussex
RH18 5ES

www.rudolfsteinerpress.com

Published by Rudolf Steiner Press 2002
New edition 2018

Rudolf Steiner's verses are selected from the following
volumes of the *Rudolf Steiner Gesamtausgabe* ('GA'), his
Collected Works published in the original German by
Rudolf Steiner Verlag, Dornach: GA 40 *Wahrspruchworte*,
GA 261 *Unsere Toten*, GA 267 *Seelenübungen* and GA 268
Mantrische Sprüche. This authorized volume is published by
permission of the Rudolf Steiner Nachlassverwaltung,
Dornach

A catalogue record for this book is available from the British
Library

ISBN 978 1 85584 548 0

Typeset by DP Photosetting, Aylesbury, Bucks.
Printed and bound in Great Britain by 4Edge Ltd., Essex

Contents

Whoever passes the door of death
dissolves into the elements,
gazes on dark midnight's bright sun,
stands before the upper and the lower gods.

(From the Egyptian)

Introduction

The verses gathered and translated here are based on verses which Rudolf Steiner wrote to sustain and hearten people when loved ones died. I have divided them into three sections: the first contains aphoristic sayings about death in general and its possible meanings for us; the second—by far the longest—consists of verses which stress the continued links between the living and the dead, and hint at how our thoughts can help those who have left earth life; and the third is devoted to poems which express something of what the dead may experience. These three sections, I like to think, show a certain relationship between head, heart and will.

I say these translations are *based* on Steiner's verses because, like all poetry, they are strictly speaking untranslatable. I have tried to convey the sense, movement and spirit of his verses; but I wanted to avoid adhering so doggedly to the original that the result became wooden. The reader must realize, therefore, that while the poems printed here are drawn directly from Steiner's intentions and words, they have passed through the mill of an English soul.

Translating is a fascinating process; and it occurs to me that parallels might be drawn with another and greater kind of translation. I very much hope that these verses offer insight, warm sustaining hope, and will for the future; and that they help mutual understanding and interest between those living on the earth and those who have been 'carried across'—the original meaning of *translate*—into another realm of life.

Matthew Barton

I

WHAT IS DEATH?

Up to the heights of life we rise
through childhood and youth; and then
descend towards earth's final goal.
The spirit is revealed at every stage:
first spirit creates the body's strength;
then, from physical power, invisible life
releases itself enriched once more, becomes
one with what it first grew from.

In every life there lies
life's new seed:
the soul dies from the old to ripen
immortally towards the new.

Our soul is a blossom of the world
ripening divine spirit within itself.

Space is steeped in riddle upon riddle,
riddle upon riddle runs through time;
answers only come when mind
grasps itself
beyond the bounds of space, beyond
the running stream of time.

However lowly, every single
earthly human being
springs from eternity,
continually vanquishes old death
in each fresh life!

From the suffering of souls,
from the blood of slaughter,
from sacrifice and bravery,
from pain, dire misery, from death
spirit fruit will ripen when
in spirit consciousness we turn
our soul sense spirit-wards.

See the sun
at deep midnight
use stones to build
in the lifeless ground.

So find in decline
and in death's night
creation's new beginning
morning's fresh force.

Let the heights reveal
divine word of gods;
the depths sustain and nurture
the stronghold of peace.

Living in darkness
engender a sun;
weaving in substance
see spirit's bliss.[1]

II

LIVING WITH THE DEAD

As from the deep blue ground of spirit
gold stars shimmer forth,
so from the deep realms of my soul
surface strong sustaining powers.

Come to me soul,
I wait.
Come into my thoughts,
they wait.
Come into my feelings,
my I waits.

My love follows, follows you
follows you in your pain
follows you in blessed joy.

In love
on Christ's paths
may my heart seek you
may you live
in my thoughts
as I live in your soul.[2]

In the light of world thoughts
weaves the soul that was
joined with me on earth.

My soul is with you,
seeking and sensing you.
It is with you
and lives with you
in what you undertake:
our lives forever
joined in destiny.

May my soul's love strive out towards you,
may my love's purpose stream towards you.
May they bear you,
and uphold you
in heights of hope,
in spheres of love.

May my devoted love
interweave with the sleeves
of life that wrap you—
cooling all heat,
warming all cold!
Love-borne, light-graced,
live upwards now!

Through the gate of death I will
faithfully follow your soul into the spirit's
light-creating spheres of time.
In love, lessening for you earthly cold,
in knowledge, forming for you spirit light;
in thought I will remain beside you,
soothing for you scorching world heat.

Let my soul follow you into spirit realms,
follow you with the love
it cherished in earthly realms
when my eye still looked on you;
let it soothe your heat,
soothe your cold,
and so we'll live united,
not sundered by spirit gates.

May my heart's warm life
stream towards your soul
to warm your cold,
to soothe your heat
in spirit worlds.
May my thoughts live in yours
and yours in mine.

Present in spirit with you,
may love's warm power kindle
from my soul's finest spirit sense:
experiencing heat with you, soothing it;
bearing cold with you, fortifying it;
perceiving you in me,
willing me in you.

Into worlds where dwells
the soul core of your being,
I send you love—
to cool your heat
to warm your cold.
And if you feel your way towards me,
I will always be beside you.

Your will was weak.
Strengthen your will.
I send you warmth for your coldness.
I send you light for your darkness.
My love to you.
My thoughts with you.
Grow, walk on.[3]

Soul in the land of souls,
seek Christ's mercy
that brings you help,
help from spirit lands
which also stills and quietens those spirits
in whom disquiet would breed despair.[4]

I look upon you in the world of spirit
in which you are.
May my love soothe your heat,
may my love soothe your cold.
May it pierce through to you
and help you find the way
through the spirit's dark
into the spirit's light.

Into spirit's fresh fields
I'll send the true, the faithful love we found
to join us soul to soul;
May you find my thinking full
of love, when from the bright-lit lands
of spirit you turn your soul to see
what you seek in me.

You were ours
and ours you will be
when now the light of spirit
pours into your pure
devoted eye of soul.

Your thoughts' fine power
will seek in spirit worlds
to find the love that we
wish faithfully to
preserve for you.

Let heart love press its way through
to soul love,
let love warmth pour through
to spirit light;
so I approach you,
thinking with you spirit thoughts,
feeling in you world love,
willing spirit through you,
weaving oneness being.

Into your soul sleep, heart-warming,
stream my thoughts.
Sense them in your unbound I.
I wish to be beside you,
bring you from your life
the earth existence which you need
for spirit remembering.

May your soul's eyes see
into the deeper strength of my thoughts.
This is my will.
May it meet your will
in the strength of the Father
in the grace and mercy of Christ
in the light of the spirit.

Whatever awaits you
through time, through worlds,
my loving heart
with all its forces
will be beside you,
sustaining,
helping.

Watchful spirit guardians of his soul,
may your wings bring
our souls' petitioning love
to the sphere-dweller now
entrusted to your care.
So that, united with your power,
our plea may shine out, help
the soul it loves and seeks.

You who guard sphere-risen souls,
you who weave around sphere-risen souls,
spirits watching over human souls, protecting,
lovingly working out of world wisdom:
hear our plea, look upon our love
that senses spirit radiance, strives to grow
one with your helping streams of strength.[5]

Divine in my soul,
I will make space for you
in my conscious being:
You link me to all
that destiny's power has given me,
you never sunder me from
what you gave me to love:
your spirit watches over mine,
for it is also yours:
so I will watch with you,
through you, within you;
I will be strong, to acknowledge
that what you have chosen
for those who are yours
is wisdom.[6]

Here she sought spirit being
there may she find spirit being;
the thoughts of her loved ones
dwell with her.

The soul strives to resound
in harmony with ethereal tones
of spirit in which beings weave
from whose forces of will the soul's
earthly life draws aim and sense.
And often the suffering that shakes
our physical life will forge
links to spirit in our depths.

So it was with this soul—she
resonated inwardly with spirit's
ethereal sounds; patience she will surely find
and peaceful rest upon her path,
so that with inward ear she also
hears the music that she is.

When peaceful submission
pierces the soul,
the way is clear for inner spirit power
to walk on through soul trial.[7]

No boundaries separate
where spirit links sustain
light-brilliant,
love-radiant
eternal soul bonds.

So I am in your thoughts,
so you in mine.

III

WAKING TO ANOTHER LIFE

In shining spheres
I feel strength of life.
Death has woken me
from sleep, from spiritual sleep.

I will be,
and form out of myself
what shining strength
illumines in me.

In world breadths I will bear
my feeling heart, so that it grows warm
in the fire where holy forces work;

In world thoughts I will weave
my thinking, so that it grows clear
in the light where life eternally evolves;

In grounds of soul I will immerse
devoted sense, so that it grows strong
for human activities' true aims;

In God's peace I will contend
with struggles and with cares of life,
to fashion my self to higher self;

Seeking an active, work-glad peace,
sensing world being in my own,
let me fulfil the human task;

then, expectant, I may live
towards the star that guides my soul,
that shows me my place in spirit realms.

Into human souls I'll guide
sense of spirit, to willingly
waken in hearts the Easter word;

with human spirits I will think
warmth of soul, that powerfully
they may feel the risen one;

brightly in death's apparent face
shines spirit understanding's earthly flame;
and self becomes the eye and ear of worlds.

As soul I am not on the earth,
but only in water, air and fire;

in my fire I am within the planets
and the sun.

In my sun being I am
the heaven of fixed stars.

As soul I am not on the earth,
but within light, word, life;

In my life I am within planetary and sun being,
in the spirit of wisdom.

In my wisdom being I am within
the spirit of love.

I was united with all of you;
remain united within me.
We will converse
in the speech of eternal being.
We will be active
where deeds take effect,
we will weave in spirit
where human thoughts are woven
in the word of eternal thoughts.

Dwell my soul
in light-filled heights
where sun-glitter dragonflies
flutter, flit; wed
beams of warmth to living space:
remembering me they weave
strength from grief;
I sense already
how they sense me;
how they penetrate and warm me,
streaming through me.

In the weave of worlds
spirit melts
earthly weight
to future light.

The Rose Cross meditation

Ex deo nascimur
We are born out of God

In Christo morimur
We die in Christ

Per spiritum sanctum reviviscimus
We are reborn through the Holy Spirit

Notes

1 This verse is entitled 'winter solstice'.
2 For a mother, on the death of her small child.
3 For someone who committed suicide.
4 For someone who committed suicide.
5 For those killed in battle.
6 For parents whose son was killed in battle.
7 This is the first section of a longer verse entitled 'In memoriam'.

Index of first lines

My love follows, follows you, 23
My soul is with you, 26
No boundaries separate, 48
Our soul is a blossom of the world, 13
Present in spirit with you, 32
See the sun, 17
Soul in the land of souls, 35
Space is steeped in riddle upon riddle, 14
The soul strives to resound, 47
Through the gate of death I will, 29
Up to the heights of life we rise, 11
Watchful spirit guardians of his soul, 43
Whatever awaits you, 42
Whoever passes the door of death, 6
Your will was weak, 34
You were ours, 38
You who guard sphere-risen souls, 44